INNER TALK
for
A CONFIDENT DAY
A LOVE THAT WORKS
PEACE OF MIND

INNER TALK

for

A CONFIDENT DAY
A LOVE THAT WORKS
PEACE OF MIND

Dr Susan Jeffers

First published in Great Britain in 1997 by Hodder & Stoughton
A division of Hodder Headline PLC

A Coronet paperback

10 9 8 7 6 5 4

ISBN 0 340 68932 3

Printed and bound in Great Britain by
Mackays of Chatham PLC, Chatham, Kent

Hodder and Stoughton
A division of Hodder Headline PLC
338 Euston Road
London NW1 3BH

DEDICATION

A Spiritual Pep-Talk—
For the Winner that Lives Within Us All

PREFACE

Confidence is something we all seek. Most of us look to the outside world in order to find it. This rarely works. It is up to us to plant our own seeds of self-respect and watch them grow. In this way we can stand tall and participate in the world in a fulfilling and joyful way.

The powerful and loving words that you are now going to read will help you plant those seeds of self-respect. They represent the strength that lives within us all . . . the strength of our Higher Selves. They are meant to replace the negative chatter in our minds which pulls us down and stops us from being all that we want to be and doing all that we want to do. If you read *Inner Talk for Peace of Mind* often, you will notice that the negative chatter will become quieter as it is replaced by the welcome sounds of the Higher Self. And you will feel your self-esteem grow.

Remember that you do not have to believe these words for them to have a powerful effect. As you read their messages over and over again, they become automatic in your thinking and you will find yourself moving into a more confident way of being. When you can, read out loud. Intermittently, take a deep breath and imagine the words becoming a part of you. If you have the audiotape, listen to it whenever you can, such as when you are dressing, exercising, or driving to work. When you hear, speak and read these empowering thoughts, the impact is enhanced.

I suggest you read *Inner Talk for a Confident Day* first thing in the morning. Carry it with you throughout the day when courage is needed. In this way, the words will always be there to guide you to your Higher Self . . . the place where all your inner strength lies.

Let's now begin some Inner Talk for a *Very* Confident Day!

From my Higher Self to yours . . .

Susan Jeffers

Inner Talk for a *Confident Day*

Right now I am choosing to create a beautiful day. I commit to focusing on all that is wonderful within and around me. I take special notice of all the blessings in my life—the sky, the trees, good friends, good food, a compliment, a helping hand, or whatever riches are put before me. Yes . . .

I am creating a beautiful day.

I am creating a beautiful day.

I am creating a beautiful day.

Today I am feeding myself nourishing thoughts. I drown out the negativity in my mind. I drown it out with love. I listen only to the healing thoughts of my Higher Self . . . the part of me that is abundant, joyful, creative, expansive, loving and knows . . .

There is nothing to fear.

There is nothing to fear.

There is nothing to fear.

I am taking responsibility for all my reactions to anything that happens in my
life. I blame no one for how I am feeling.
I refuse to see myself as a victim. I look
for the growth that all experiences offer
me.

I am in control of my life.

I am in control of my life.

I am in control of my life.

I am careful not to blame myself. There is no need for blame at all. Instead I applaud every little step that I take in the direction of self-empowerment. With each step . . .

*I feel myself growing stronger
and stronger.*

*I feel myself growing stronger
and stronger.*

*I feel myself growing stronger
and stronger.*

I am getting in touch with the enormous power within me—power to grow, power to change, power to create joy and satisfaction in my life, power to act, power to move forward, power to love and be loved. I constantly remind myself . . .

I am powerful and I am loving.

I am powerful and I am loved.

I am powerful and I love it!

I am my own best friend. I notice all my accomplishments . . . big or small. I am proud of who I am learning to be. I pat myself on the back for how far I have come . . .

I like who I am.

I like who I am.

I like who I am.

I allow no one to take away my good feelings today. I am attracting positive people into my life. I commit to surrounding myself with loving, energetic, giving, caring human beings who support the best that I am.

I surround myself with love.

I surround myself with love.

I surround myself with love.

I stand tall in the face of any negative energy that tries to pull me down. No matter what is happening around me, I take a deep breath and remember that I learn from all life experiences. I look for the opportunity for growth in every situation that I encounter.

I feel centered and whole.

I feel centered and whole.

I feel centered and whole.

As I feel abundant, riches flow into my
life. So much within me. So much around
me. I breathe deeply and keep my heart
open to receive all the riches before me.

*I am drawing to me all
good things.*

*I am drawing to me all
good things.*

*I am drawing to me all
good things.*

Today I am learning to trust. Most importantly I trust who I am. And who I am is someone who is capable of creating all the true riches of the Universe . . . friends, joy, satisfaction, fulfillment.

I am creating all that I need.

I am creating all that I need.

I am creating all that I need.

I trust that I can handle whatever happens in my life. I can handle illness. I can handle losing money. I can handle getting older. I can handle failure. I can handle success. I can handle rejection. I can handle being alone. I can even handle the loss of people I love. Yes . . .

Whatever life hands me,
I'll handle it!

Whatever life hands me,
I'll handle it!

Whatever life hands me,
I'll handle it!

I practice letting go today, surrendering to the Higher Power that lives within and around me. I create without worry. I do what needs to be done and I release my fear about the outcome.

I let go and I trust.

I let go and I trust.

I let go and I trust.

I trust my instincts . . . messages from my Higher Self. I listen to the voice within that knows everything it needs to know. I trust the Universal Wisdom that always knows the Grand Design. Easily and effortlessly . . .

I am being shown the way.

I am being shown the way.

I am being shown the way.

I am moving forward with confidence and love. Each day my trust in myself increases. I can feel my confidence grow. I am capable of creating much more than I ever thought possible.

I am alive with possibility.

I am alive with possibility.

I am alive with possibility.

Today I am taking at least one risk into the unknown. With each step forward I become stronger and more confident. I expand my ability to handle my fears. I take only those kinds of risks that have integrity and love behind them. I am careful not to infringe on the rights of others, nor to do bodily harm to myself.

*I act responsibly and lovingly
toward myself and others.*

*I act responsibly and lovingly
toward myself and others.*

*I act responsibly and lovingly
toward myself and others.*

I have all the energy to do everything that needs to be done. I tap into my infinite source of Inner Strength. I move into life with excitement and commitment.

*I was born to use my
loving power.*

*I was born to use my
loving power.*

*I was born to use my
loving power.*

Today I commit 100% to all areas of my life. When I am at work, I am there 100%. When I am with family and friends, I am there 100%. I continually ask myself, if I were truly important here, what would I be doing? And I do it.

*I know that I count . . . and I
act as if I do.*

*I know that I count . . . and I
act as if I do.*

*I know that I count . . . and I
act as if I do.*

I am learning to give from a place of love rather than expectation. There is so much abundance in my life, that I can let go and begin giving it away. I need never hold back.

In giving, I feel fulfilled.

In giving, I feel fulfilled.

In giving, I feel fulfilled.

Today, I take the time to truly care. I reach out and touch. I open up to the pain in other people's live and respond with compassion.

I touch . . . and my life is touched.

I touch . . . and my life is touched.

I touch . . . and my life is touched.

Today I am focusing on something bigger than myself. I am part of a bigger whole. I say yes to the opportunity to get involved in the process of making ours a peaceful planet. I am already a success. I am creating a better world in whatever I do . . . at home, at work and at play. In everything I do . . .

I light the fire that warms the world around me.

I light the fire that warms the world around me.

I light the fire that warms the world around me.

There is so much excitement and wonder in my life. Sometimes I experience the ecstasy of being in the flow. Sometimes I experience the agony of being way off course. It is all part of the process of living and learning. I always remember . . .

It is all happening perfectly.

It is all happening perfectly.

It is all happening perfectly.

I nod my head up and down instead of side to side. I let go of my resistance and allow in new possibilities. I relax my body and calmly survey each situation. I delight in the opportunity to taste all that life has to offer . . . the bitter along with the sweet.

I say "YES!" to it all.

I say "YES!" to it all.

I say "YES!" to it all.

I am supported by the positive energy of the Universe. I take a leap into faith and soar. I know I can do it . . . be it . . . enjoy it. I am living a successful life. I am following the Divine within me.

I am on the right Path.

I am on the right Path.

I am on the right Path.

As my mind aligns with my Higher Self . . . I trust. I appreciate. I love. I care. I am at peace. I am creative. I count. I make a positive difference. I give. I receive. I am involved. I am content. I live now. I am helpful. I am joyful. I forgive. I am relaxed. I am alive. I am powerful. I am protected. I let go. I am aware of my blessings. I am connected. I am excited. I am confident. And I know . . .

There is nothing to fear.

There is nothing to fear.

There is nothing to fear.

On the following pages, write those Inner Talk messages that speak to you most powerfully at this moment in your life. Or, begin creating your own Inner Talk for a Confident Day.

INNER TALK FOR A CONFIDENT DAY

INNER TALK FOR A CONFIDENT DAY

INNER TALK FOR A CONFIDENT DAY

INNER TALK FOR A CONFIDENT DAY

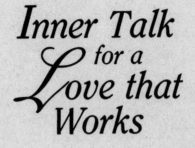

Inner Talk
for a
Love that
Works

DEDICATION

To the Miracles—
That Love Brings into our Lives

♥ ♡ ♥

PREFACE

It is my joy to bring to you some powerful Inner Talk that will help you take charge of Love. The words you are now going to read are about creating greater closeness with that special person in your life. If you are not in a romantic relationship, apply the messages to someone close to you—a friend, a parent, a child, a co-worker. It's good practice. After all, love is love . . . with whomever we find it!

The aim of these positive messages is to help replace any negative thoughts you may hold about your past, present or future relationships with the empowering thoughts of the Higher Self, the best of who you are. As you do, you will understand what it truly means to honor yourself . . . and others.

Remember, you do not have to believe these words for them to have a healing effect. Trust that, at some level, their message is being heard.

Ideally, this book should be read daily for at least one month . . . or until the words become automatic in your thinking. As you read, intermittently take a deep breath to allow the body to relax into the warming energy that is being created. When you can, say the words out loud. If you have the audiotape, listen to it whenever you can, such as when you are lying in bed, exercising or dressing. When you hear, speak and read these positive thoughts, the impact is enhanced. You can also carry the book with you throughout the day to be used whenever you want to remind yourself what a "Higher" love looks like.

As you read *Inner Talk for a Love that Works* over and over again, you will slowly learn how to live into a life filled with love.

From my Higher Self to yours,

Susan Jeffers

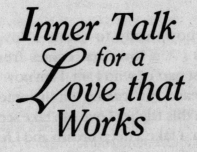

Inner Talk
for a
Love that Works

I am now ready to create a love that works . . . a love that comes from the highest part of who I am. I am now ready to create the caring environment in which this Higher Love can take seed and bloom. I take a deep breath and I feel my loving energy grow.

To guide me on this path of love with the special person now in my life . . . or with someone I will one day meet . . . I affirm the following words from the best of who I am . . .

I am healing the inner hurts that stop me from loving myself and loving you.

I am letting go of negative emotions that keep me separated from love.

I am letting go of the need to blame . . . myself or you.

I am transforming my neediness into authentic caring.

I am taking action to create a rich and nourishing life.

I am surrounding myself with people who bring me joy.

I am learning to trust that I am a person of worth.

I am pulling up the great power that resides within me.

I am opening my heart to love.

I am opening my heart to love.

I am opening my heart to love.

I now take the time to look at those emotions that separate me from love. I look first at any anger I may be holding toward people in my life . . . past or present. I release them of all blame knowing that blame is a powerless act.

Instead I accept my anger as a sign that it is now time for me to take control of my actions and reactions in life. To channel my anger into a positive tool of self-discovery and self-healing, I affirm the following words that come from the Power Within . . .

I am sculpting my life the way I want it to be.

I have choice in my life.

I am now taking action.

I have nothing to fear.

I am reclaiming my power.

With an open heart, I move out of the way of those who try to hurt me.

I see their inner pain and lovingly let them go.

I am drawing nourishing people into my life.

♥ ❤ ♥

*I am creating a life filled
with love.*

*I am creating a life filled
with love.*

*I am creating a life filled
with love.*

♥ ♡ ♥

As I release others from blame, I am careful not to blame myself. I know that all my experiences are a source of growth and learning.

♥ ♡ ♥

No matter what has happened in my life,
I lovingly affirm the following . . .

There are no mistakes . . . only opportunities for growth.

I stand tall and take responsibility for my life.

I am worthy of dignity and love.

I am a lover-in-training and I am learning my lessons well.

I am learning something valuable from all life experiences.

I follow my Inner Light that leads the way to love.

♥ 🖤 ♥

I trust who I am.

I trust who I am.

I trust who I am.

♥ ♡ ♥

I am now creating a safe space for greater intimacy to occur. I understand that we are both doing the very best that we can to share our truth with one another.

♥ ❤ ♥

To help keep the feeling of closeness alive, I affirm the following . . .

I am your friend.

I am on your side.

I am sending you thoughts of love.

I listen to and I hear what you have
to say.

I open my heart to receive.

I accept all your actions as your desire to
be loved.

I see the beauty within you.

♥ ♡ ♥

I am letting in your love.

I am letting in your love.

I am letting in your love.

♥ ♡ ♥

I pick up the mirror and look at my need
to be right . . . my need to always have
the last word. I now know I am good
enough. I love and respect all of who
I am.

There is nothing I have to prove . . . to you or to me. With confidence in myself, I lovingly affirm the following . . .

I open up to hear what you have to say.

I respect your point of view as I respect
my own.

I see in you much of what I need to learn.

From the level of the Soul, we are One.

I love you.

I love you.

I love you.

I now learn the meaning of trust. I know that the only thing I can safely trust is my ability to handle whatever you say or do to me.

We are both human and cannot predict the future. When I fully trust myself, the fear goes away, and what's left is the love.

♥ ♡ ♥

I trust who I am.

I handle whatever happens in my life.

I am cutting the cord of dependency.

My self-esteem is growing every day.

I am creating a beautiful life.

I trust the future.

There's always more.

I am strong and I am whole.

I am strong and I am whole.

I am strong and I am whole.

I now release all my negative judgments. I let go of my anger and fear and appreciate what is truly wonderful about you. I am learning how to take as I acknowledge and appreciate what you bring into my life . . . no matter how big . . . no matter how small.

♥ ♡ ♥

I feel surrounded by abundance as I affirm the following words from my
Higher Self . . .

♥ ♡ ♥

I thank you for the many things you do for me.

I thank you for your many acts of kindness.

I thank you for sharing so many wonderful moments.

I thank you for the times you think about me.

I thank you for what I learn about myself through you.

I thank you for listening and loving and caressing and cajoling and laughing and trying and hoping and caring and being and doing and buying and supporting and sharing and helping and nurturing and protecting and walking the walk and talking the talk.

I thank you for being a part of my life.

Thank You.

Thank You.

Thank You.

In order to truly love you, it is essential that I learn to love who I am. To love who I am means to know in my mind, to feel in my heart, and to reflect into this world my Inner Beauty, my Inner Strength, and my Inner Light.

I pick up the mirror and focus on all the beauty that lies within my Body, Mind and Soul. In my actions and in my words, I lovingly remind myself that at the level of my Highest Self . . .

I am filled with a vibrant Living Force.

I am capable and whole.

I am a responsible person.

I am powerful and I am loving.

I am a pleasure to know.

I am filled with beauty, strength and light.

My life makes a difference.

I touch the world wherever I go.

I have so much to give.

I hold my head up high.

I deserve love.

I love who I am.

I love who I am.

I love who I am.

♥ ♡ ♥

As I learn to love who I am, I support you in learning to love who you are.

I always let you know through my actions and my words that at the level of
your Highest Self . . .

♥ ♡ ♥

You are filled with a vibrant Living
Force.

You are capable and whole.

You are a responsible person.

You are powerful and you are loving.

You are a pleasure to know.

You are filled with beauty, strength and
light.

Your life makes a difference.

You touch the world wherever you go.

You have so much to give.

You can hold your head up high.

You deserve love.

I love who you are.

I love who you are.

I love who you are.

I let go of fairy tale expectations that set me up for disappointment. The only expectation I have of this relationship—or any relationship, whether it lasts one week, twenty-five years, or until death do us part—is that I will learn more about opening my heart and becoming a more loving person.

I am a Lover-in-Training. To create a love that works requires awareness and practice. I commit to taking those steps that guide me toward a Higher Love. To keep me on the path, I affirm the following . . .

My being a loving person depends only on me.

I am creating an inner energy of love that touches everyone around me.

I am warming the world with my love.

My life makes a difference.

The love in my life begins with me.

I love who I am.

I am pulling up the Great Power within me.

♥ ♡ ♥

I am opening my heart to love.

I am opening my heart to love.

I am opening my heart to love.

♥ ♡ ♥

To create a Higher Love, I know I must be a lover of humanity. The more I become a "lover" in the world outside my relationship, the more I can be a lover inside my relationship.

♥ ♡ ♥

I remind myself over and over again, I am needed to bring more love into this world. There are so many people who would welcome my love.

I am reaching out to those around me.

I am inviting others into my life.

My eyes say, "Welcome."

My smile says, "I would like to know you better."

My heart says, "I care."

*I embrace the world like a
lover!*

*I embrace the world like a
lover!*

*I embrace the world like a
lover!*

I begin each day by asking myself, "If I were really important in this home, this community, and this world, what would I be doing? And I do it . . . one step at a time.

♥ ♡ ♥

With each step that I take, I live into the full awareness of my Higher Purpose in life . . .

My Higher Purpose is to ease someone's pain.

My Higher Purpose is to care.

My Higher Purpose is to share.

My Higher Purpose is to give.

My Higher Purpose is to have compassion.

My Higher Purpose is to project light wherever I go.

*I warm the world with my
love.*

*I warm the world with my
love.*

*I warm the world with my
love.*

On the following pages, write those Inner Talk messages that speak to you most powerfully at this moment in your life. Or, begin creating your own Inner Talk for a Love that Works.

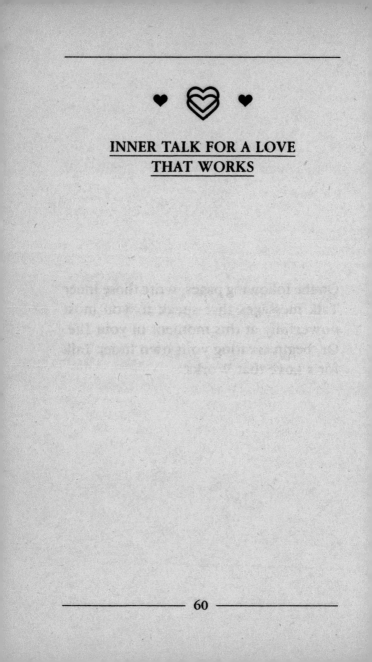

INNER TALK FOR A LOVE
THAT WORKS

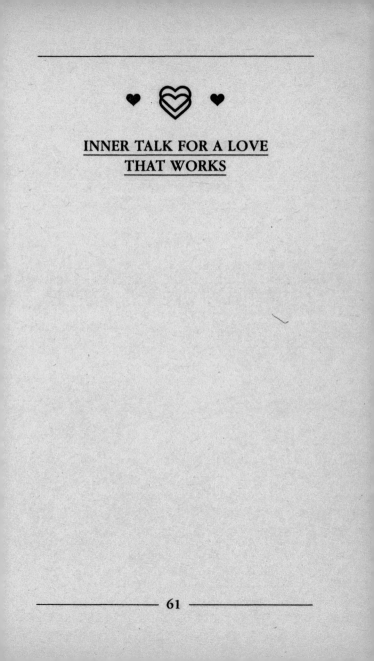

INNER TALK FOR A LOVE
THAT WORKS

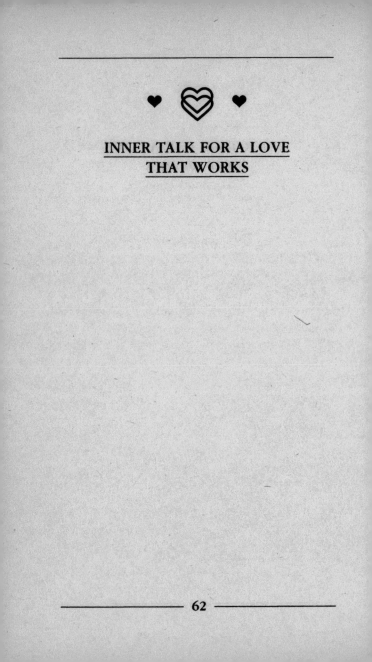

INNER TALK FOR A LOVE
THAT WORKS

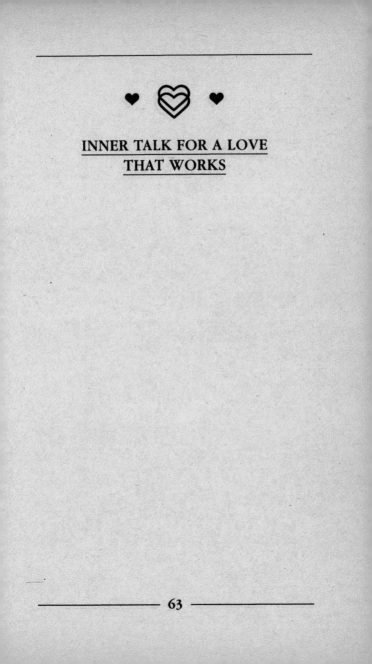

INNER TALK FOR A LOVE
THAT WORKS

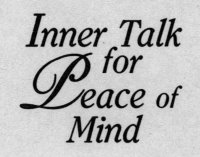

Inner Talk for
Peace of
Mind

DEDICATION

A Lullaby—
For the Fearful Child
That Lives Within Us All

PREFACE

We live in a very stressful world. And the child within us is often afraid. Yet, despite what is going on in our lives, it is possible to find the place within that is powerful and loving and knows there is nothing to fear. This is the place of the Higher Self.

I wrote *Inner Talk for Peace of Mind* to help you get in touch with the voice of your Higher Self. Most of us hear only the voice of doom and gloom. The negative chatter in our minds pulls us down and makes us feel vulnerable. It makes us want to control everyone and everything around us. The voice of our Higher Self, on the other hand, can soothe our fears by letting us know that we are safe and that we can handle anything that happens to us in life.

The comforting words that you are now going to read represent the power and love that live within us all. If you read them daily, they will ultimately replace the negativity in your mind. Remember that you do not have to believe these words for them to have a powerful effect. As you read their messages over and over again, they become automatic in your thinking and you will find yourself moving into a more peaceful state of mind.

When you can, say the words out loud. Intermittently, take a deep breath to allow the body to relax into their healing thoughts. Read *Inner Talk for Peace of Mind* just before you go to bed. Then, if you have the audiotape, let it lull you to sleep. When you hear, speak and read these soothing messages, the impact is enhanced. Carry the book with you throughout the day to be used when you feel stressed. Its message will help you feel centered and calm, will help you transcend petty upsets, and will help you find the best of who you are. In this way, you will always have a guide to your Higher Self . . . the place where all your Inner Peace lies.

From my Higher Self to yours,

Susan Jeffers

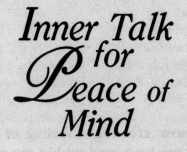

Inner Talk
for
Peace of
Mind

I am now creating a feeling of peace within my body and within my mind. I take a deep breath and feel myself relax. From the top of my head to the tip of my toes . . .

I feel the tension melting away.

I feel the tension melting away.

I feel the tension melting away.

I take another deep breath and let the light from my Higher Self enter every cell of my being. I feel the warmth soothing all places of upset and stress.

I am bathed in healing light.

I am bathed in healing light.

I am bathed in healing light.

I take still another deep breath and relax into the arms of my Higher Self. I feel the safety and caring that my Soul radiates. I surrender to its magnificent strength. I am cradled with love and . . .

I am safe.

I am safe.

I am safe.

I now close the door to the past. I trust
that whatever has happened in my life is
a teaching for my highest good. I trust
that I am finding the gift of wisdom from
all my life experiences. I leave the dark-
ness behind and I move forward into the
flow of love and light.

I am filled with love and light.

I am filled with love and light.

I am filled with love and light.

I release my fears about tomorrow. I am on the right path. I am doing all that needs to be done. I am guided every step of the way. I relax. I am safe.

*My life is unfolding in a
perfect way.*

*My life is unfolding in a
perfect way.*

*My life is unfolding in a
perfect way.*

I rise above any matters that try to pull my attention away from all that's good in my life. I stop obsessing about anything that tries to take away my peace. I realize that what is truly important, above all else, is the love I give to myself and others.

What is important is the love.

What is important is the love.

What is important is the love.

I give up my need to control everything within and everything around me. I surrender to the Eternal Wisdom that fills my being. I listen carefully knowing that the answer always appears.

*I trust the Wisdom that
lies within.*

*I trust the Wisdom that
lies within.*

*I trust the Wisdom that
lies within.*

I let go of my worry about money. I release all thoughts of scarcity. There is always enough. I am capable of creating everything I need. I move into the light and see the huge expanse of possibility.

Life is an exciting adventure.

Life is an exciting adventure.

Life is an exciting adventure.

I let go of trying to control other people's lives. I trust that they, too, are learning exactly what they need to learn. I trust that they, too, walk the path toward their Higher Self . . . in their own way and in their own time.

*Life is happening perfectly . . .
for all of us.*

*Life is happening perfectly . . .
for all of us.*

*Life is happening perfectly . . .
for all of us.*

Although I live in a world of strife, I remain in the place of peace. I hold fast to the light of my Soul. I move my attention from my head to my heart. From this place I see things clearly. And from this place I know . . .

There is nothing to fear.

There is nothing to fear.

There is nothing to fear.

I trust that all is happening for my Highest Good, despite how it might appear. I trust that I am learning and growing from all life experiences. I let go of trying to control the outcome of all situations in my life.

I let go and I trust.

I let go and I trust.

I let go and I trust.

I trust that the perfect plan is unfolding. As the seeds blossom into a beautiful garden, so, too, my life is blossoming into overflowing abundance . . .

*I peacefully allow my life
to unfold.*

*I peacefully allow my life
to unfold.*

*I peacefully allow my life
to unfold.*

I trust myself. Within me is an endless source of energy that will handle all that needs to be handled. I push away all self-doubt and replace it with self-love. I constantly remind myself . . .

I am worthy of love.

I am worthy of love.

I am worthy of love.

I am finding a solution to all tasks set before me. I ask my Higher Self to show me the way and I relax knowing I have it within me to handle all that needs to be handled.

*I trust the miracle of my
Higher Self.*

*I trust the miracle of my
Higher Self.*

*I trust the miracle of my
Higher Self.*

I remind myself over and over again that, in all manner of things, I need not worry. I need not fret. I am doing everything that needs to be done . . . exactly when it needs to be done.

One step at a time is enough for me.

One step at a time is enough for me.

One step at a time is enough for me.

I am whole . . . Body, Mind and Soul. I
need no one else to complete me. I cut
the cord that makes my survival depen-
dent upon anyone or anything else. I
know I am a powerful being.

I now claim my Inner Strength.

I now claim my Inner Strength.

I now claim my Inner Strength.

Each day I am learning. Each day I open the door wider . . . the door that leads me to my Higher Self. I have the Inner Strength to find my way.

I am finding my way.

I am finding my way.

I am finding my way.

I put aside all stressful thoughts and focus
on the beauty of the now. The flowers,
the sunsets, the caring, the touching of
each other's lives. I open up to take in all
the gifts that have been given me. Life is
abundant. I trust that I am in loving hands
and I know that . . .

All is well.

All is well.

All is well.

I am getting my priorities straight. What is most important is the love and warmth that I bring to the world. My life has meaning. My life has purpose. Every day I am learning more about becoming a loving person. The rest is unimportant. The rest is just part of the drama.

*The only thing that matters is
the Love.*

*The only thing that matters is
the Love.*

*The only thing that matters is
the Love.*

I lighten up about life. Everything I do is perfect for my growth and self-discovery. I love my life and I am ready to receive all the gifts that are being offered me. I am deeply grateful for my many blessings. Life is truly grand.

I welcome it all.

I welcome it all.

I welcome it all.

I ease up on myself. I need not rush. I let go and allow the river to carry me to new adventures. I obey the laws of Eternal Rhythm. There is plenty of time for me to do everything I need to do. I constantly remind myself . . .

There is plenty of time.

There is plenty of time.

There is plenty of time.

I feel the light of my Higher Self as an everpresent beacon leading the way. I tune into the Wisdom of my Higher Self. I ignore any doubts inside my head.

*I am filled with peaceful
awareness.*

*I am filled with peaceful
awareness.*

*I am filled with peaceful
awareness.*

I am at peace. I imagine the warmth of the sun upon my face. I realize that my Higher Self is connected to a Universal Light that warms this world. I draw the Light into me and now gently send this Healing Light back into the world.

I am a source of Healing Light.

I am a source of Healing Light.

I am a source of Healing Light.

I am at peace. All the weights are now being lifted from my shoulders. I feel calm. I feel free. I let in the Loving Light of the Universe. I feel the warmth course throughout my body. I become the Light.

*I touch the beauty of
who I am.*

*I touch the beauty of
who I am.*

*I touch the beauty of
who I am.*

I pull up the Great Power that resides within me. The loving arms of my Inner Light envelope me and keep me safe. I feel nurtured. I let go of any need to control anything or anyone around me and I trust that no harm shall befall me.

I am at peace.

I am at peace.

I am at peace.

On the following pages, write those Inner Talk messages that touch you most powerfully at this moment in your life. Or, begin creating your own Inner Talk for Peace of Mind.

INNER TALK FOR PEACE OF MIND

INNER TALK FOR PEACE OF MIND